MW00896113

A GUIDE TO DR. MINDY PELZ'S BOOK

WORKBOOK

FAST LIKE A GIRL

A WOMAN'S GUIDE

TO USING THE HEALING POWER OF FASTING
TO BURN FAT, BOOST ENERGY, AND BALANCE HORMONES

PEAKREAD PUBLISHING

© Copyright 2023 by PeakRead Publishing – All rights reserved.

The purpose of this document is to provide precise and dependable information on the subject matter and issues addressed herein. It should be noted that the publication is sold with the understanding that the publisher is not obligated to provide accounting, legally authorized, or other qualified services. If professional or legal advice is required, it is recommended that an individual with expertise in the relevant field should be consulted.

It is important to note that the aforementioned principles were approved by a committee of the American Bar Association and a committee of publishers and associations. Moreover, it is strictly prohibited to reproduce, duplicate, or transmit any part of this document in any form, whether electronically or in print. Recording of this publication is also prohibited, and any storage of this document is not allowed without written permission from the publisher. All rights are reserved.

The information contained in this publication is represented to be truthful and consistent. Any liability, in terms of negligence or otherwise, arising from the use or abuse of any policies, processes, or instructions contained within is the sole responsibility of the recipient reader. In no event shall the publisher be held legally responsible for any damages, compensation, or monetary loss caused by the information contained in this publication, whether directly or indirectly.

The copyrights to this publication are owned by the respective authors, not the publisher. The information provided herein is for informational purposes only and is universal in nature. The presentation of the information is not intended to create a contract or guarantee.

The trademarks used in this publication are without any consent or permission from the trademark owners. The use of these trademarks is not endorsed or backed by the owners of the trademarks. The trademarks and brands referenced in this publication are solely for clarification purposes and are owned by their respective owners, not affiliated with this document.

Disclaimer/Terms of Use: The product names, logos, brands, and other trademarks mentioned in this publication are the property of their respective trademark holders and are not affiliated with Knowledge Tree. The publisher and author of this publication make no representations or warranties with respect to the accuracy and completeness of the contents contained herein and disclaim all warranties, including warranties of fitness for a particular purpose. This guide is unofficial and unauthorized, and it is not authorized, approved, licensed, or endorsed by the original book's author, publisher, or any of their licensees or affiliates.

For information regarding bulk purchases, special editions, and subsidiary rights, please contact PeakRead Publishing at: **peakreadpublishing@gmail.com**

Published by: PeakRead Publishing

First Printing: June 2023

ISBN: 979-8397415170

Interior Design: PeakRead Publishing

Printed in United States of America

Cover image: Image by Freepik

MAKE THE CHANGE, NOT ONLY FOR YOURSELF!

DONATION OPPORTUNITY

Fasting instills a deep sense of empathy and understanding. As we momentarily experience the absence of sustenance, we become acutely aware of the privilege of having access to nourishment. We recognize that our temporary sacrifice has the potential to create a lasting impact in the lives of those less fortunate.

To embody the true essence of this revelation, we are proud to announce that a portion of every purchase of this workbook will be dedicated to a noble cause close to our hearts: feeding the poor. With each workbook sold, we take a step towards uplifting communities, one nourishing meal at a time.

Imagine the satisfaction of knowing that your personal growth journey is intertwined with a larger purpose – the opportunity to make a meaningful difference. By joining forces with us, you are not only embracing the power of fasting but also extending a helping hand to those who need it most.

Together, we can break the cycle of hunger, forging a brighter future for individuals who have been burdened by scarcity. Through your support, we will partner with reputable organizations and initiatives especially those in 3rd world countries, channeling our collective efforts to ensure that no one goes to bed hungry.

This is not just a book; it is a catalyst for change. As you embark on your path toward personal empowerment, you can rest assured that your purchase has a ripple effect beyond the pages. Let us unite, nourishing not only our bodies but also the souls of countless individuals in need.

Join the movement. Be a force for good. Together, let's make a lasting impact on the lives of the less fortunate. With this workbook in your hands, you have the power to transform not only yourself but also the world around you.

Feed your soul and feed the poor. Your journey begins here.

DISCLAIMER

We would like to inform you that this summary and analysis workbook of "The Body Keeps the Score: Brain, Mind, and Body in the Healing of Trauma" is a plagiarism-free resource created to complement your original reading experience, not to substitute it.

Our intention in producing this summary and analysis workbook is to provide you with a helpful tool that can enrich your understanding and engagement with the original book. It is not intended to replace the original source material, which we highly recommend you purchase and read in its entirety.

We strongly encourage you to purchase the original book, by scanning the QR code below, you will be directed directly the Amazon:

YOUR FREE GIFT!

Thank you for your recent purchase!

Enjoy a free set of our top-selling workbooks as a token of our gratitude.

Scan the QR code below to download them and unlock valuable tips, exercises, and exclusive offers.

WORKBOOK OVERVIEW

Embark on a transformative journey towards optimal health with the workbook companion to the book "Fast Like a Girl" by Dr. Mindy Pelz.

This comprehensive workbook is a powerful tool designed to help you revolutionize your approach to women's health.

By embracing the principles of fasting, hormone balancing, and energy enhancement, you can reclaim your well-being and unlock your full potential. Through engaging journaling exercises, reflective activities, and guided practices, this workbook empowers you to take charge of your health and embark on a path of self-discovery.

Inside this workbook, you will:

- Master the art of fasting: Learn how to fast like a pro, discovering the profound benefits of giving your body a break from constant digestion. Acquire the knowledge and techniques to implement fasting effectively and safely.

- Achieve hormone balance: Support your hormones with simple yet powerful tips and tricks that can bring newfound balance to your body. Uncover strategies to optimize hormonal health and enhance overall well-being.

- Explore ancestral healing: Delve into the ancient practice of ancestral healing, tapping into the wisdom of your predecessors to unlock your full potential. Discover how connecting with your ancestral roots can positively impact your health and well-being.

- Harness your body's innate intelligence: Gain a deep understanding of your body's unique needs and learn how to work harmoniously with its innate intelligence. Cultivate a profound connection with yourself as you develop strategies to support your body's natural healing processes.

- Boost metabolic health: Uncover proven techniques that will revitalize your metabolism, leaving you feeling energized and revitalized. Take proactive steps towards improving your metabolic health and achieving long-lasting vitality.

More than just a compilation of tips and tricks, this workbook is a transformative journey of self-discovery. It invites you to tune in to your body's needs, tap into your inner health warrior, and embrace a new paradigm of women's health. Get ready to elevate your well-being and embark on a fulfilling path towards optimal health and vitality.

TABLE OF CONTENTS

INTRODUCTION

OVERVIEW OF FAST LIKE A GIRL

Fast Like a Girl by Dr. Mindy Pelz is an all-encompassing book that serves as a comprehensive guide for women aiming to enhance their metabolic health through fasting.

Dr. Pelz, an experienced chiropractor, certified nutritionist, and fasting expert, draws upon her extensive patient care expertise spanning over two decades to provide valuable insights and practical advice.

Divided into three parts, the book delivers a deep understanding of the scientific aspects surrounding female hormones, principles of food that support metabolic well-being during fasting, and personalized fasting options tailored to individual lifestyles.

In the first part, Dr. Pelz explores the role of female hormones such as estrogen, progesterone, and testosterone in the body and their interaction with fasting. She offers valuable insights into how the menstrual cycle impacts fasting and provides specific tips for fasting during each phase. Emphasizing the importance of women adopting a distinct fasting approach from men, she ensures that readers can achieve a high-quality fasting experience.

The second part of the book focuses on food principles that prevent metabolic disturbances while fasting. Dr. Pelz highlights that fasting alone is insufficient and underscores the significance of maintaining a balanced diet. Introducing the concepts of ketabiotic and hormone feasting, she guides readers on building well-rounded plates that incorporate healthy fats, quality proteins, and nutrient-rich carbohydrates.

The third part of the book caters to readers' individual lifestyles by presenting personalized fasting options. Dr. Pelz presents a 30-day Fasting Reset program encompassing various fasting protocols, including intermittent fasting, extended fasting, and time-restricted eating. Moreover, she offers practical advice on adjusting fasting schedules to accommodate specific circumstances such as shift work or travel.

Throughout the book, Dr. Pelz supports her recommendations with scientific evidence, highlighting the benefits of fasting such as improved gut health, strengthened immune system, and increased production of happiness hormones. Additionally, she conscientiously warns readers about potential risks associated with fasting, such as nutrient deficiencies, emphasizing the importance of approaching fasting protocols with caution.

Fast Like a Girl stands out with its dedicated focus on women's health, recognizing the significance of tailoring fasting practices to accommodate hormonal differences. Dr. Pelz provides specific guidance for fasting during different phases of the menstrual cycle and offers recommendations for women navigating menopause.

The book maintains a conversational and accessible tone, making complex scientific concepts easily understandable for readers. Dr. Pelz supplements her expertise with personal anecdotes from her own fasting journey and includes compelling case studies from her patients to illustrate key points effectively.

Overall, Fast Like a Girl is a practical and informative resource that offers valuable guidance on fasting and metabolic health for women. Dr. Pelz's evidence-based recommendations highlight the importance of customizing fasting approaches to individual needs, making the book suitable for women of all ages and fitness levels who seek to improve their overall health and energy levels.

HOW TO USE IT

The "Fast Like a Girl" workbook is a valuable resource that equips women with a wide range of tips and strategies to successfully integrate fasting into their daily lives.

Designed to support women in achieving their fasting goals, this comprehensive guide provides essential information and tools necessary for a fulfilling fasting journey.

To effectively utilize the workbook, follow these steps:

Introduction and Familiarization: Begin by reading the introduction to understand the purpose and structure of the workbook. Familiarize yourself with its format and how each section is organized.

- Section-by-Section Approach: The workbook is divided into several sections, each containing chapters that explore different aspects of fasting. Take your time to read and absorb the content of each chapter, paying attention to the central ideas and strategies presented.

- Chapter Summaries and Lessons Learned: After reading each chapter, review the corresponding chapter summary and lessons learned section. This step reinforces your understanding of the material and helps solidify key takeaways.

- Reflective Questions: Each chapter offers a set of questions meant to facilitate introspection and self-reflection. Engage with these questions to deepen your understanding and gain insights into your personal fasting journey. You can record your answers or even discuss them with fellow readers or members of your fasting community.

- Journaling and Writing Prompts: The provided questions can serve as writing prompts for journaling. Use them to document your progress, challenges, and successes throughout your fasting journey. Regularly journaling will help you stay focused, motivated, and accountable.

- Form a Fasting Group: Consider forming or joining a fasting group with other women who are also utilizing the "Fast Like a Girl" workbook. Meeting regularly with this group to discuss progress, share tips and strategies, and offer support can be incredibly beneficial in maintaining motivation and accountability.

By following the suggestions and strategies outlined in the workbook, you can achieve your fasting goals and experience the benefits of a healthy, balanced lifestyle. The workbook serves as an invaluable resource, guiding you step-by-step toward successful fasting integration and empowering you to make positive changes in your life.

YOUR VISION

Dear Reader,

These blank pages have been intentionally left empty to provide you with a space where you can reflect on your journey as you read through the book. Use this space to write down your goals, intentions, and aspirations for this journey. You can also take some time to reflect on your past experiences and how they have impacted your life.

By jotting down your thoughts and feelings, you will be able to compare your growth and progress at the end of this book. This workbook is designed to help you gain a deeper understanding of yourself and how to use fasting to your advantage. Take advantage of this opportunity to create a roadmap for your healing journey.

Remember, this is your personal journey, and there is no right or wrong way to go about it. Allow yourself to be vulnerable, and embrace the process with an open mind. We hope that this workbook serves as a helpful tool in your healing journey.

Best of luck,

"PeakRead Publishing" Team

_____

PART ONE: THE SCIENCE

CH 1: IT'S NOT YOUR FAULT

Summary

The initial chapter of the book, titled "It's Not Your Fault," commences with a concise elucidation of the intricate interplay of cells, nutrients, and hormones within the intricate framework of the human body.

The author astutely highlights the staggering existence of over thirty-trillion cells meticulously toiling in harmony to sustain your very existence. With each instance of nourishment, your body diligently assimilates the nutrients derived from the food and diligently dispatches them to these intricate cellular entities. Circling each cell is a discerning receptor, which possesses the capacity to open and close in response to the hormonal dynamics within your body, thereby permitting or restricting the entry of these vital biochemical messengers into the cellular realm.

The book astutely recognizes that numerous dietary regimens often neglect the essential consideration of cellular functioning and hormonal balance. In fact, these regimens have the potential to impede and disrupt the inherent natural processes of cells and hormones. The author conscientiously acknowledges five pivotal mistakes frequently encountered in dieting endeavors that may inadvertently cause more harm than good, both in terms of weight loss goals and overall well-being. The quintet of dieting missteps encompasses the following:

Diets that restrict calories / Diets with low-quality food / Diets that do not address cortisol / Diets that do not limit toxins / Diets that are not tailored to the individual

The first type of diet that the author astutely recognizes as problematic is the one that imposes restrictions on calorie intake. The book perceptively highlights the prevailing misconception among many individuals who perceive calorie counting as the ultimate key to achieving and maintaining a slim physique. However, the author astutely reveals that this prevailing belief is not entirely accurate. It is elucidated that each person possesses a unique threshold of calories necessary to sustain a consistent weight, which is commonly referred to as the "set point." The author discerningly explains that when one consumes fewer calories than their body's set point, the body gradually adapts to this reduced caloric intake and subsequently adjusts the set point accordingly. Regrettably, this adjustment does more harm than good, as it necessitates a further reduction in calorie consumption to sustain continuous weight loss.

To substantiate these assertions, the author substantiates their claims by referencing the noteworthy Minnesota Starvation Experiment, which was conducted in the 1960s. This compelling study involved the participation of 36 men who were subjected to a significantly diminished caloric intake to examine the effects of starvation. Upon the culmination of the experiment, the participants reported a notable deterioration in their mental well-being and an unexpected 10% increase in their body weight compared to their pre-experiment measurements.

Moving forward, the subsequent detrimental diet strategy addressed within the contents of this book pertains to the consumption of poor-quality food. The author perceptively observes that low-fat and fat-free food options have gained significant popularity as perceived health-conscious choices. However, it is crucial to recognize that these seemingly virtuous options may not be as nutritionally beneficial as they initially appear. The author astutely elucidates that low-fat and fat-free food products often incorporate the addition of sugars to enhance their palatability. Regrettably, the consumption of these added sugars prompts the body to produce heightened levels of insulin to facilitate their processing. Prolonged exposure to excessive insulin impedes the body's ability to efficiently process both insulin and sugar.

Consequently, the body commences storing the surplus insulin and sugar as adipose tissue, commonly known as fat. This intricate process, referred to as insulin resistance, paradoxically hampers weight loss endeavors and counteracts the desired outcomes.

Moving onward, the author diligently confronts the third diet-related predicament, which revolves around the escalation of cortisol levels. Cortisol, a hormone discharged by the body during periods of heightened stress, becomes a focal point of concern.

It is crucial to recognize that when cortisol levels surge, they trigger a concurrent increase in insulin production. As expounded upon by the author in the earlier discourse regarding dietary problems, elevated insulin levels can lead to an array of complications. The surge in cortisol can occur as a consequence of stress-inducing circumstances, including calorie restriction, as previously discussed.

However, it is imperative to acknowledge that cortisol spikes can transpire due to factors unrelated to food, such as excessive physical exertion, work-related challenges, or tumultuous interpersonal relationships. Additionally, the author thoughtfully underscores that women exhibit a higher susceptibility to stress compared to men.

Consequently, any well-rounded and beneficial dietary approach should diligently tackle this issue and strive to alleviate cortisol levels to promote optimal well-being.

Yet another perilous dietary approach that receives due attention in the book pertains to the presence of toxins. When toxins infiltrate our bodies, our cells possess the ability to store them as a protective measure, often in the form of fat. The author astutely advocates for a paradigm shift in our perception of fat, emphasizing its potential role in safeguarding our well-being.

Within the realm of toxins, the book duly acknowledges several of the most detrimental culprits, including BPA plastics, phthalates, atrazine, organotins, and perfluorooctanoic acids (PFOA). Nevertheless, it is crucial to comprehend that these are merely a select few among the multitude of toxins to which our bodies may be exposed. The author conscientiously acknowledges that the book does not encompass an exhaustive analysis of all the toxins pervasive in our environment, but rather chooses to concentrate on toxins present in our food supply.

To illustrate this point, the author provides two compelling examples of toxins found in food: monosodium glutamate and soy protein isolates. These examples serve as a starting point to shed light on the toxic elements that may infiltrate our diets. Moreover, the author prudently recognizes that chapter six of the book will delve further into the exploration of additional food toxins, underscoring the comprehensive nature of the upcoming discussions on this crucial topic.

Concluding this chapter, the author delves into the final counterproductive aspect of diets, namely the failure to customize them according to individual needs. In support of this notion, the book highlights the distinct requirements of two crucial hormones found in women: estrogen and progesterone.

These hormones possess contrasting preferences when it comes to dietary composition. Estrogen tends to fare well with a low-carbohydrate diet, while progesterone leans towards a diet comprising a higher carbohydrate content.

The author astutely emphasizes the significance of considering women's natural hormonal cycles when designing any dietary approach. Furthermore, the author advocates for the indispensability of tailoring diets to suit the unique requirements of each individual, recognizing the inherent diversity in physiology, metabolism, and personal health goals.

To conclude the inaugural chapter on a poignant note, the author shares the inspiring narrative of Sarah, an individual who valiantly battled with poor health for an extended period. After mustering the determination to assume control over her well-being, Sarah fortuitously stumbled upon the author's enlightening YouTube videos.

Motivated by newfound knowledge, Sarah embarked on a fasting regimen meticulously tailored to her specific health needs. The profound impact of this dietary transformation became evident as Sarah shed an astonishing 80 pounds and astounded her doctors with her significantly improved health. Sarah's story serves as a powerful testament to the potential benefits of aligning diet with individual requirements and illustrates the transformative impact that informed dietary choices can have on one's well-being.

LESSONS AND KEY POINTS FROM THIS CHAPTER

1. It is important to recognize that many dietary approaches fail to adequately account for the specific needs of women, thereby potentially causing more harm than good.

2. By imposing calorie restrictions, diets inadvertently train the body to adapt to a lower caloric intake, which can impede weight loss efforts and make it more challenging to achieve desired results.

3. The consumption of low-fat and fat-free food products, despite being perceived as healthier options, can result in insulin resistance due to the inclusion of added sugars, thereby compromising metabolic function.

4. In times of heightened stress, the body releases cortisol, which can have a detrimental impact on weight loss endeavors by influencing various physiological processes.

5. Toxins introduced into the body are often stored as fat, underscoring the critical importance of eliminating toxins from the diet in order to facilitate effective weight loss.

6. Women possess a distinct hormonal profile, and therefore, their diet should be tailored accordingly to optimize their hormonal balance and overall well-being, acknowledging the varying dietary needs dictated by different key hormones.

REFLECTION QUESTIONS

What foods do you suspect are detrimental to your health, despite being advertised as healthy?

Have you ever experienced feelings of sadness or anxiety as a result of following a particular diet?

What are your aspirations in your journey towards achieving optimal health and well-being?

MILESTONE GOALS

1. What are some toxins you should avoid?

2. Are low-fat and fat-free foods as healthy as they sound?

3. What is a set point, and how does it change when you restrict calories?

4. What increases cortisol?

ACTIONABLE MOVEMENTS

1. Stop focusing solely on calorie restriction and instead focus on nutrient-dense whole foods. Start by making small changes to your diet, such as adding more fruits and vegetables and reducing the intake of processed foods.

2. Avoid ultra-processed foods that are high in added sugars, unhealthy fats, and refined carbohydrates. Instead, choose whole foods that are rich in nutrients and fiber.

3. Practice stress-reducing activities, such as deep breathing exercises, to help manage cortisol levels and prevent spikes in glucose levels.

4. Avoid consuming foods that contain harmful obesogens, such as BPA plastics, phthalates, atrazine, organotins, and PFOA. Check labels and choose organic and natural foods as much as possible.

5. Finally, shift your focus towards positive and sustainable habits, rather than obsessing over numbers on a scale. Embrace a holistic approach to health and wellness that includes regular physical activity, stress management, quality sleep, and a balanced diet.

Record your reflections, insights, and observations on the concepts discussed earlier.

Use this space to brainstorm, sketch, or jot down any questions that arise in your mind. Make it a truly personal experience.

CH 2: THE HEALING POWER OF FASTING

Summary

In Chapter Two, titled "The Healing Power of Fasting," the author delves into a comprehensive exploration of three primary focal points:

1. A glimpse into the historical origins of fasting and its contemporary manifestation.
2. An elucidation of the manifold benefits associated with fasting.
3. An examination of the diverse types of fasting and the unique advantages they offer.

The author astutely acknowledges that fasting has become relatively uncommon in modern times. However, it was an integral part of the lifestyle embraced by our prehistoric ancestors. In those bygone eras, the availability of sustenance fluctuated in accordance with food supplies, hunting success, and gathering opportunities, giving rise to cycles of feast or famine.

Interestingly, some scientists hypothesize the existence of a "thrifty gene" embedded within our DNA that thrived on this pattern of alternating abundance and scarcity. Although fasting may not be as prevalent in present-day society. Ramadan is a prime example of fasting in the modern age. Ramadan is a religious fast. However, this type of fast, like any other, can have many health benefits for participants.

The author lists many benefits of fasting. These benefits are:
- **Increased Ketones -** When our bodies can't get energy from sugar, they turn to stored fat, which they process through ketones. Another benefit of fasting is

autophagy. This process literally means self-cleaning and is the process cells use to clean and repair themselves.

- **Breakdown of glycogen -** When our bodies get too much sugar, this sugar gets stored as glycogen. The most common places for bodies to store glycogen are in the muscles, liver, and fat. By fasting, our body is forced to use this glycogen for energy, improving the function of these organs.

- **Production of the growth hormone -** The growth hormone helps us stay young, build muscles, burn fat, and support the brain. While our bodies stop producing this hormone around thirty years of age, fasting can stimulate the production of this hormone again.

- **Dopamine production -** Dopamine is a feel-good hormone and can be produced whenever we eat. However, we can become addicted to increased dopamine levels and use food to literally feed this addiction. Fasting helps to reset dopamine levels and break this addiction. Support the immune system - Studies of cancer patients have shown that taking a water fast of 72 hours helps the body to clear out old white blood cells and replace them with new, healthy white blood cells.

- **Support gut health -** The author notes that there are ten times the amount of bacteria in the gut as human cells in the body. This bacteria is crucial for the digestive system to function properly. But antibiotics, stress, and certain foods can kill off this gut microbiome. Antibiotics are especially harmful as 90% of our gut biome can be killed by just one round of antibiotics. However, fasting gives your natural microbiome a chance to replenish and your GI system to function like new again.

- **Prevent recurrence of cancer -** The book cites a 2016 study published in the Journal of The American Medical Association. In this study of two thousand women who had beaten cancer, the results found a 64% reduction in the likelihood of these women developing breast cancer again after fasting for at least thirteen hours.

After addressing the benefits of fasting, the author moves on to the five types of fasting. Each type of fasting lasts for a different length and can offer unique health benefits. These five types of fasting are:

#1. Intermittent Fasting
Take yourself through what a day without food for 17 hours might look like. You can start at 7 p.m. and eat again around 10 a.m. which is a 15-hour fast.

Somewhere between the 12-15 hour mark, ketones will flood your bloodstream, which will go to your brain and turn off your hunger needs. This will begin to move you towards a state of autophagy.

This type of fasting is a great entry point to fasting and will help you begin to change your body so that it burns fat rather than sugar.

You can start by either delaying breakfast or moving your dinner up by an hour, whichever works best for you. Some reasons you may start intermittent fasting include:
• The desire to lose weight
• If you experience brain fog
• Loss of energy

Weight Loss. There are many people who have lost weight simply by engaging in 15-hour fasts.

Brain Fog. As you fast, ketones will go to your brain around 15 hours. This will help you experience mental clarity.

Loss of Energy. Because different meals provide different kinds of energy, you will notice that when you fast, your body will derive energy from your fat, giving you the zing you might get from caffeine, without the negative jitters.

#2. Autophagy Fasting
Autophagy fasting is like a dim switch that starts around the 17-hour mark of fasting and brightens up the most around the 72-hour mark.
Do this fasting when you want to:
• Detox
• Improve brain function
• Prevent a cold
• Balance sex hormones

Detox. You should definitely detox if you've taken a vacation where you've overindulged. Doing so will help you reset your system.

Improve brain function and cognition.
Autophagy fasting helps improve:
• Memory recall
• Mental cognition
• Mental clarity and focus

Prevent a COLD. When you fast and enter a state of autophagy, new bacteria and viruses can't replicate.

Balance Sex Hormones. A key root cause of polycystic ovary syndrome (PCOS) is from dysfunctional autophagy. Fasting helps with the challenges from this sickness.

#3. Gut-Reset Fast (24+ hours)

This fast will trigger a burst of stem cells to release to your gut and repair inner mucosal lining. This fast is also the first point where your body will produce new stem cells.

This fast can:
- Counteract antibiotic use
- Offset birth control use
- Help tackle small intestinal bacterial overgrowth

Counteract Antibiotic Use. Because antibiotics can change your microbial system in your gut, fasting will help undo the damage that antibiotics may have caused, even after years of damage.

Offset Birth Control. Use Birth control can cause leaky gut, which a 24-hour fast can heal much better than a fancy diet or pill.

Help Tackle SIBO. A sign of this stubborn sickness is bloating when you eat fibrous foods like vegetables. A 24-hour reset will help your gut reach a state of homeostasis, so it can function optimally.

#4. Fat-Burner Fast (36+ hours)

Lean into this fast to:
- Minimize weight-loss resistance
- Release stored sugar
- Reduce cholesterol

Minimize Weight-Loss Resistance. A study of alternate-day fasting (ADF) found that it helped people's body's release sugar to improve weight loss.

Reduce Cholesterol. Doing this 36-hour fast will clean your liver lower your cholesterol levels.

#5. Dopamine-Reset Fast (48+ hours)

Fasting longer than 24 hours will make your dopamine receptors more sensitive. Doing so for over 48 hours will help in the weeks after you have fasted by:
- Rebooting dopamine levels
- Lowering your anxiety levels

Reboot Dopamine. Levels Our dopamine levels can become saturated and make it difficult to enjoy life. Just one 48-hour fast can help reset your ability to enjoy dopamine the way it was meant to be enjoyed.

Lower Anxiety Levels. Fasting for this length of time will help stimulate your prefrontal cortex and help your brain make the neurotransmitter GABA. You will feel much calmer at the 48-hour mark.

#6. Immune-Reset Fast (72+ Hours)
Try this fast to:
- Ease a chronic condition
- Prevent chronic disease
- Alleviate pain and stiffness
- Slow down the effects of aging

Ease a Chronic Condition. This fast is especially helpful for those with cancer, unrelenting autoimmune conditions, stubborn musculoskeletal injuries, and lifestyle-induced type 2 diabetes.

Prevent Chronic Disease. Fasting helps your immune system stay strong and prevents cancerous cells from growing.

Alleviate Relentless Musculoskeletal Injuries. The author tested this type of fast to help her with an Achilles tendon injury that wouldn't go away. She did a five-day fast to heal, and it worked like a charm.

Anti-aging. Going past the 72-hour mark of fasting stimulates stem cells that help repair your body. The next chapter will go into the concept of metabolic switching.

This second chapter ends with encouragement from the author that fasting is a personal exercise and women should learn about fasting to find the system that best supports them. The author promises to continue with a more thorough explanation of the considerations of fasting, like metabolic switching, unique hormone profiles, and how to vary the length of fasts.

LESSONS AND KEY POINTS FROM THIS CHAPTER

1. The author sheds light on the historical context in which our ancestors frequently engaged in fasting, driven by the inherent dynamics of their hunter-gatherer lifestyle.

2. Fasting is revealed to offer a multitude of profound health benefits, underscoring its potential as a transformative practice for holistic well-being.

3. The chapter delves into an insightful examination of the varying lengths of fasting and the unique array of health benefits associated with each duration.

4. Recognizing the individuality of each woman's physiological and lifestyle factors, the

book encourages women to discover and embrace the fasting schedule that resonates best with their unique needs and preferences.

REFLECTION QUESTIONS

What are the different uses and benefits of fasting?

What are the six different fasting lengths and what are their uses?

Moving forward, how do you plan to use fasting to your benefit? Are there specific situations or conditions you would like to address when fasting?

What conditions ail you currently? Imagine yourself in a better state; what does that look like to you?

MILESTONE GOALS

1. What is a modern-day example of fasting?

2. What is the benefit of fasting you want to see in your life?

3. Which of the five types of fasts is most aligned with your health goals?

4. How will you tailor fasts for your lifestyle and health goals?

ACTIONABLE MOVEMENTS

1. Start with intermittent fasting: Intermittent fasting is the most accessible and popular type of fasting, which involves fasting for 12-16 hours. Start by delaying breakfast or moving your dinner up by an hour, whichever works best for you. Intermittent fasting is a great entry point to fasting and will help you begin to change your body so that it burns fat rather than sugar.

2. Try longer fasts: After you've tried intermittent fasting and feel comfortable with it, you can try longer fasts such as autophagy fasts, gut-reset fasts, fat-burner fasts, dopamine-reset fasts, and immune-reset fasts.

3. Exercise on an empty stomach: When you're in a fasted state, your body switches to fat-burning mode, which can help you burn more calories during exercise. Exercise can also help you get through your fast by keeping your mind off food.

4. Stay hydrated: Drink plenty of water, herbal tea, and other non-caloric beverages to stay hydrated during your fast.

5. Eat a healthy diet: When you're not fasting, make sure to eat a healthy diet consisting of whole, nutrient-dense foods. This will help support your body during fasting periods and provide the nutrients your body needs for optimal health.

6. Track your progress: Keep track of how you feel during and after fasting periods. This will help you determine what type of fasting works best for you and how often you should fast.

Consult a healthcare professional: If you have any medical conditions or concerns, consult a healthcare professional before starting any fasting regimen. They can help you determine what type of fasting is safe for you and provide guidance on how to do it properly.

Record your reflections, insights, and observations on the concepts discussed earlier.

Use this space to brainstorm, sketch, or jot down any questions that arise in your mind. Make it a truly personal experience.

CH 3: METABOLIC SWITCHING: THE MISSING KEY TO WEIGH LOSS

Summary

Continuing the narrative, Chapter Three, titled "Metabolic Switching: The Missing Key to Weight Loss," builds upon the anticipation set at the conclusion of Chapter Two, now centering its focus on the concept of metabolic switching. The author astutely highlights a captivating fact that our bodies undergo a remarkable renewal process every seven years, during which all our cells are replaced. While this may initially sound like promising news, the author elucidates that if our cells are already compromised or diseased, this replication merely perpetuates the proliferation of unhealthy cells. Consequently, the imperative need for metabolic switching arises as a means to restore cellular health.

The book goes on to provide a comprehensive explanation of metabolic switching—a crucial physiological process through which our bodies seamlessly transition between utilizing glucose and ketones as sources of fuel.

Recalling the earlier chapters, it becomes apparent that ketones play a pivotal role in the body's utilization of stored fats and sugars for energy. Notably, our ancestors frequently experienced metabolic switching as they navigated a lifestyle characterized by feast or famine, adapting their fuel sources based on the availability of food. However, in the modern era, food is abundantly accessible, and the experience of genuine metabolic switching has become increasingly rare among many individuals.

This is especially concerning as metabolic switching has a host of health benefits. These health benefits are:

- **Switching between autophagy and mTOR**
- **Hormetic stress**
- **Mitochondria healing**
- **Regenerate neurons**

The first noteworthy advantage of metabolic switching lies in its ability to facilitate a dynamic interplay between autophagy and mTOR in the brain. Autophagy serves as the cellular process responsible for cleansing and rejuvenation, while mTOR represents cell growth.

The book emphasizes that frequent eating can elevate mTOR levels, accelerating cell growth and consequently shortening cell lifespan. Conversely, fasting can reduce mTOR levels, but excessive fasting may lead to undesirable outcomes such as muscle breakdown. Therefore, metabolic switching assumes paramount importance as it enables the body to leverage both autophagy and mTOR for optimal cellular functioning.

The second significant benefit associated with metabolic switching, as highlighted in the book, relates to hormetic stress. This form of stress encompasses mild, controlled stress that enhances the adaptability of cells. As cells become more adaptable, they also exhibit improved health and efficiency.

Our bodies possess a remarkable capacity to adapt to patterns, underscoring the importance of periodically altering fasting routines and dietary patterns to sustain the beneficial effects of hormetic stress.

Drawing a parallel, the book draws attention to how weightlifters often modify their workout routines to prevent their muscles from plateauing. Similarly, through hormetic stress, metabolic switching facilitates similar adaptability and resilience within our cells. Another compelling advantage discussed in the book regarding metabolic switching pertains to its ability to facilitate the healing of mitochondria. As you may recall from previous scientific or health-related studies, mitochondria serve as the powerhouses of our cells, playing a vital role in energy production and cellular detoxification.

Notably, organs such as the heart, liver, brain, eyes, and muscles boast a particularly rich concentration of mitochondria. Groundbreaking research conducted by Thomas Seyfried, published in the journal Cancer as a Metabolic Disease, has shed light on a significant revelation: there is mounting evidence suggesting that the onset of cancer originates from dysfunctional mitochondria, rather than solely from genetic factors, as was previously believed.

Intriguingly, unhealthy mitochondria exhibit a preference for ketones (energy derived from stored fats and sugars) over glucose, owing to the unique assistance that ketones provide to these vital cellular structures in two distinct ways:

1. Ketones help mitochondria produce glutathione, a master antioxidant that helps the cell detox.

2. Ketones help the mitochondria with the methylation process. Through this process, toxins are pushed out of cells. Since sick mitochondria do not produce enough glutathione and do not methylate efficiently, providing ketones as fuel to the mitochondria helps this cell powerhouse heal itself.

The ultimate advantage attributed to metabolic switching lies in its remarkable capacity to facilitate neuronal regeneration within the brain. Neurons, being highly vulnerable to damage caused by inadequate nutrition, exposure to toxins, and insufficient utilization, face the risk of degeneration, which can be a precursor to conditions such as Alzheimer's disease.

However, metabolic switching emerges as a potent ally in combating the decline of neurons. The author highlights inspiring examples of women in their fifties experiencing heightened mental acuity, surpassing their cognitive abilities in their thirties, all attributable to the effects of metabolic switching.

Having delved into the various benefits of metabolic switching, the book proceeds to address the specific health concerns that metabolic switching can effectively alleviate.

These noteworthy health concerns encompass:

1. Aging: One of the remarkable benefits of metabolic switching is its ability to enhance cellular adaptability, thereby promoting overall cellular health. Moreover, studies have demonstrated that alternate-day fasting can upregulate the SIRT1 gene, renowned for its anti-aging properties.

2. Weight Loss: By compelling the body to utilize stored fats and sugars as sources of energy, metabolic switching becomes a powerful ally in the pursuit of weight loss.

3. Memory Problems: The brain comprises two distinct types of cells, with approximately 50% relying on glucose for energy and the other 50% favoring ketones. Metabolic switching ensures that brain cells receive an energy supply from both sources, thereby potentially benefiting memory-related concerns.

4. Reduced Risk of Cancer: Since cancer often originates from dysfunctional mitochondria, fasting provides an opportunity for these vital cellular structures to undergo repair. Additionally, metabolic switching aids in the elimination of toxins through autophagy. It is important to note that when individuals embark on fasting, they may initially experience symptoms such as brain fog, bloating, diarrhea, constipation, and low energy as the body eliminates excess toxins. In Chapter Ten, the book explores strategies to alleviate these symptoms.

5. Autoimmune Conditions: Autoimmune conditions can arise from various factors such as gut-related issues, toxin accumulation, or genetic predispositions. Metabolic switching presents a potential avenue for improving all these underlying causes of autoimmune conditions.

Chapter Three delves into the comprehensive exploration of metabolic switching, elucidating its definition and unveiling the extensive array of benefits associated with this transformative process.
Furthermore, this chapter diligently attends to five distinct health concerns that can be significantly ameliorated through the practice of metabolic switching.

With a firm grasp on the underlying scientific principles surrounding fasting and metabolic switching, the chapter concludes by promising readers an enlightening journey on the practical application of these techniques in their own lives, customized according to their unique hormonal requirements.

LESSONS AND KEY POINTS FROM THIS CHAPTER

1. The natural process of cell replacement occurs approximately every seven years, making it essential to prioritize the maintenance of cellular health. By ensuring that our cells are in optimal condition, they can replicate into a newer generation of healthy cells.

2. Metabolic switching serves as the mechanism through which our bodies seamlessly transition from utilizing glucose as the primary source of fuel to relying on ketones for energy production.

3. Metabolic switching offers a multitude of profound health benefits, encompassing the ability to alternate between autophagy and mTOR, harnessing hormetic stress, promoting mitochondrial healing, and facilitating the regeneration of neurons.

4. In addition to its wide-ranging advantages, metabolic switching demonstrates remarkable potential in addressing various health concerns such as the effects of aging, weight loss management, memory-related issues, cancer prevention, and the management of autoimmune conditions.

REFLECTION QUESTIONS

How do you plan on being conscious of the healing process while fasting?

What are some signs that your detox pathways are clogged?

In what ways do you plan to use hormetic stress to give your body the ability to adapt and not stay overly comfortable?

MILESTONE GOALS

1. What is hormetic stress?

....

....

....

2. What two ways do ketones help the mitochondria of cells?

....

....

....

3. How do autophagy and mTOR differ? How do these two processes work together?

....

....

....

4. What are ketones?

....

....

5. Do the cells in your brain prefer glucose or ketones for fuel?

ACTIONABLE MOVEMENTS

1. Start with a plan: Begin by creating a fasting plan that works for you. There are different types of fasts, such as intermittent fasting, extended fasting, and time-restricted eating, and it is essential to choose one that you can stick to.

2. Start slow: If you are new to fasting, start with shorter fasts, such as intermittent fasting for 12-16 hours or time-restricted eating for 8-10 hours. Gradually increase the length of your fasts over time.

3. Combine fasting with a healthy diet: When you break your fast, make sure to eat nutrient-dense, whole foods that support your body's health. Avoid processed foods, refined sugars, and other unhealthy options that can negate the benefits of fasting.

4. Vary your fasts: As mentioned in the chapter, varying your fasts can create hormetic stress that encourages your body to become metabolically stronger. Consider alternating between different types of fasts, such as intermittent fasting, extended fasting, and time-restricted eating.

5. Listen to your body: Pay attention to your body's signals, and if you feel unwell during your fast, stop and eat. If you have any underlying medical conditions, consult your healthcare provider before starting a fasting plan.

6. Stay hydrated: Drink plenty of water during your fasts to stay hydrated and support your body's detoxification processes.

7. Combine fasting with exercise: Regular exercise can support your body's metabolic switching and overall health. Consider incorporating light exercise during your fasting period, such as walking.

By following these steps, you can implement the principles of metabolic switching through fasting to promote weight loss, improve mitochondrial function, repair your gut health, slow down the aging process, and provide mental clarity. Remember to be patient, as these benefits may take time to manifest, and always listen to your body's needs.

Record your reflections, insights, and observations on the concepts discussed earlier.

Use this space to brainstorm, sketch, or jot down any questions that arise in your mind. Make it a truly personal experience.

CH 4: FASTING A WOMAN'S WAY

Summary

In the fourth chapter entitled "Fasting a Woman's Way," the author introduces us to the remarkable journey of Bridget. At the age of forty-two, Bridget found herself facing the frustrating challenge of weight gain, despite diligently adhering to her tried-and-tested diet and exercise routines. Desperate for a solution, Bridget turned to fasting as a potential remedy.

Over the course of six months, she witnessed remarkable progress and significant improvements while incorporating fasting into her lifestyle. However, after this initial period, Bridget encountered unexpected symptoms, such as anxiety, panic attacks, and hair loss.

Seeking answers and guidance, Bridget consulted her doctor, who advised her to discontinue fasting, asserting that it was not suitable for women. Undeterred, Bridget embarked on a quest for knowledge and discovered enlightening resources, including the author's enlightening YouTube videos. Empowered by the author's insights and recommendations, Bridget resumed her fasting practices, attaining the same remarkable health benefits she had experienced previously, but this time without any adverse effects.

The triumph and transformation Bridget achieved serve as a testament to the invaluable information shared in this pivotal fourth chapter. Within its pages, the author imparts three crucial takeaways for readers to embrace and apply to their own fasting journeys:

1. Personalized fasting: Recognizing the significance of your unique hormonal cycle, it is essential to tailor your fasting practices accordingly. Understanding how your hormones fluctuate throughout different phases of your cycle can optimize the benefits you derive from fasting and promote better overall well-being.

2. Hormonal hierarchy: Delving into the intricate workings of your hormones and their collective impact on your body and health, the author emphasizes the importance of comprehending the hormonal hierarchy. Unveiling the interplay and influence of various hormones, this knowledge empowers you to navigate your fasting journey more effectively and unlock its full potential.

3. Tailored approach for women: Acknowledging the inherent physiological differences between men and women, the author underscores the significance of adopting a distinct approach to fasting that caters specifically to the needs and nuances of the female body. By recognizing these distinctions and embracing a gender-specific fasting strategy, women can optimize their fasting experience and harness its transformative effects.

In the quest to unravel the intricate relationship between fasting and the hormonal cycle, the author provides readers with a guided tour through the typical 28-day menstrual cycle, keeping in mind that each woman's cycle length may vary. While 28 days is the most common duration, it serves as a representative framework for understanding the interplay of hormones. Let's delve into the fascinating details:

The journey begins with the first ten days of the menstrual cycle, during which testosterone and progesterone levels are at their lowest. It's important to note that estrogen gradually builds up in the body, reaching its peak around day thirteen. Recognizing the manifold benefits of estrogen, such as promoting healthy skin, strengthening bones, and supporting ligaments, the author highlights this phase as an opportune time to tackle emotionally challenging tasks.

Moving forward, the cycle enters the ovulation period, spanning from approximately day ten to fifteen. During this phase, both estrogen and testosterone assume pivotal roles. Women often experience a sense of empowerment during this time, thanks to the influence of these hormones. Consequently, it becomes an ideal window to embark on new projects, conquer arduous tasks, or take on a heavier workload. Moreover, the heightened presence of testosterone facilitates muscle building, making strength training a particularly effective exercise during this period.

As the cycle progresses from day sixteen to eighteen, testosterone production continues to increase, which may result in reduced energy levels and a slightly clouded mental state. It's essential to be mindful of these physiological changes and adjust one's activities and expectations accordingly during this phase.

By grasping the nuances of the hormonal fluctuations throughout the menstrual cycle, individuals can tailor their fasting approach accordingly. Recognizing the varying impacts of hormones at different stages empowers women to optimize their fasting practices, align their activities with their hormonal dynamics, and leverage the distinctive strengths associated with each phase of their cycle.

The fourth phase of the menstrual cycle extends from approximately day nineteen until the onset of bleeding. During this period, many women experience a sense of calmness and desire a more relaxed schedule. It is important to note that progesterone reaches its peak six to eight days after ovulation and plays a crucial role in preparing the uterine lining for potential fertilization.

The production of progesterone relies on the hormone dehydroepiandrosterone (DHEA). Given that cortisol negatively impacts DHEA levels, it becomes essential to minimize stress during this phase. Consequently, the author advises against fasting during this stage to prevent a spike in cortisol.

Having covered the different phases of the hormonal cycle, the author proceeds to explain the concept of the hormonal hierarchy. In this hierarchy, insulin takes center stage as the controller of progesterone, estrogen, and testosterone. Conversely, insulin is influenced by cortisol, thereby establishing a direct link between the two hormones. At the pinnacle of this hierarchical structure resides oxytocin, commonly referred to as the feel-good hormone. In summary, the hormonal hierarchy can be described as follows:

1. Oxytocin
2. Cortisol
3. Insulin
4. Progesterone, Estrogen, & Testosterone

These hormones are all related because of the hypothalamus and pituitary in the brain. The hypothalamus notes the hormones in the body and tells the pituitary what other hormones should be created. Since oxytocin is at the top of the hierarchy, it is crucial to support this hormone. Oxytocin can be supported by deep breathing and expressing gratitude...etc

The final takeaway from this chapter is why women need to fast differently than men. One reason for this is that men have only a twenty-four-hour hormonal cycle, whereas women have a (roughly) twenty-eight-day cycle. Another reason for fasting differences is due to toxic loads. Toxins are heavily impacted by hormone production. When hormones shift, toxins stored in the body can be released. In fact, the CDC notes that pregnant women release lead in their bones due to changes in hormones.

These differences are why many women have vastly different experiences fasting than men. The author closes with a story of Jude, who started fasting with her husband. Only Jude did not have the same positive experience as her husband. Instead, she gained weight and became anxious. By learning about her hormonal cycle, the hormonal hierarchy, and the fasting needs of women versus men, Jude was able to change her fasting schedule and see the same positive effects of fasting as her husband.

LESSONS AND KEY POINTS FROM THIS CHAPTER

1. Women experience a hormonal cycle that typically spans 28 days, although the duration may vary among individuals. In contrast, men have a 24-hour cycle. Consequently, it is important for women to adapt their eating and fasting patterns according to the different phases of their menstrual cycle.

2. The menstrual cycle of a woman consists of four distinct phases. These phases include days 1-10 characterized by lower levels of testosterone and progesterone, days 10-15 known as the ovulation period, days 16-18 when testosterone reaches its peak, and days 19 until the onset of bleeding when progesterone levels are at their highest.

3. The hormonal hierarchy involves the intricate interaction of six key hormones. Within this hierarchy, oxytocin assumes the highest position, influencing and regulating the other hormones.

4. Women possess a unique hormonal cycle distinct from men, and they also exhibit a heightened susceptibility to toxins. Considering these differences, it is crucial for women to take them into consideration when engaging in fasting practices.

REFLECTION QUESTIONS

What happens during the four stages of the menstrual cycle?

What do you think you should take note of when fasting along your cycle?

What are the different functions of your hormones?

What do you think you will need to do as you fast because of how each hormone reacts differently?

MILESTONE GOALS

1. During what phase of your cycle should you not fast? What is the reasoning for not fasting?

_____

_____

_____

2. How can you support oxytocin production and help your hormonal hierarchy?

_____

_____

_____

3. When in your cycle is it best to take on more work or start a difficult project?

_____

_____

_____

4. What can cause stored toxins in the body to be released?

_____

_____

_____

5. What hormone directly controls progesterone, testosterone, and estrogen?

_____

_____

ACTIONABLE MOVEMENTS

1. Understand your menstrual cycle: Women should track their menstrual cycles to understand their length, hormonal fluctuations, and the different stages they go through during their cycle.

2. Sync fasting with the menstrual cycle: Based on the understanding of the menstrual cycle, women can start syncing their fasting regimen with their menstrual cycle. They can fast differently at different stages of their cycle to align with their hormone fluctuations.

3. Plan fasting periods: Women can plan their fasting periods ahead of time based on their menstrual cycle. For instance, during the follicular phase (day 1-10), women can consider fasting as their estrogen and testosterone levels are low. During ovulation (day 11-15), intermittent fasting is recommended. During the luteal phase (day 16-18), all hormones dip, and fasting can be more challenging. Women should avoid fasting the week before their period (day 19-28) as progesterone is susceptible to disrupting glucose and cortisol levels.

4. Consider the impact of toxic loads: During times of high hormone levels, women should consider shorter fasting lengths to avoid toxins from being released into the bloodstream. It is also essential to listen to your body and adjust your fasting regimen accordingly.

5. Balance hormones: Women should also work towards balancing their hormones by reducing stress, managing cortisol levels, and taking steps to improve thyroid function. A healthy diet and exercise can also help balance hormones and improve overall well-being.
By implementing these steps, women can optimize their fasting regimen, improve their overall health, and reduce stress during their menstrual cycle.

Record your reflections, insights, and observations on the concepts discussed earlier.

Use this space to brainstorm, sketch, or jot down any questions that arise in your mind. Make it a truly personal experience.

PART TWO: THE ART OF FASTING LIKE A GIRL

CH 5: BUILD A FASTING LIFESTYLE UNIQUE TO YOU

Summary

Chapter five, titled "Build a Fasting Lifestyle Unique to You" marks the beginning of the second part of this book "The Art Of Fasting Like a Girl". Within this chapter, the author addresses the prevalent issue of healthcare being predominantly approached as a generic solution for everyone. However, there is a growing recognition and adoption of personalized healthcare, often referred to as functional medicine. The roots of this concept can be traced back to Hippocrates, the founding figure of medicine, who tailored his treatments based on the individual's age, physique, and constitution.

In the modern era, functional medicine embraces the n-to-1 approach, where patients actively participate in the decision-making process regarding their treatment options. Applying this principle to fasting, the author urges readers to adopt a similar mindset. To customize fasting to align with one's specific goals, the author highlights four essential pillars that should be taken into consideration when devising a fasting protocol.

1. Identify your fasting goals / 2. Switch up your fasting lengths / 3. Eat a variety of foods / 4. Build a community with other fasters

The first pillar of fasting involves determining one's specific goals. According to the author, many people have three common objectives when fasting: weight loss, hormone balance, and addressing specific conditions. It's worth noting that achieving hormone balance through fasting may require a period of at least ninety days. To gain insights into individual hormone levels, a urinary hormone test can be beneficial.

The next pillar emphasizes the importance of varying fasting lengths. The author recommends aiming for an eight-hour eating window as a base fasting schedule. However, to prevent plateaus and promote progress, incorporating longer fasts is necessary. It's crucial to take into account the natural hormonal cycle when scheduling these extended fasting periods. Additionally, fasting should be adaptable to accommodate social events, vacations, holidays, and other personal commitments.

The third pillar of fasting focuses on diversifying food choices. The author highlights that many women tend to consume the same thirty foods regularly.

However, maintaining gut health and hormone balance requires dietary variety. Interestingly, the types of gut bacteria present can influence cravings. When only a limited range of foods is consumed, specific gut bacteria thrive and can trigger cravings. By introducing a wider array of foods into the diet, a greater diversity of gut bacteria can flourish, leading to reduced cravings.

The fourth and final pillar of fasting emphasizes the importance of building a supportive community. The author encourages readers to seek out a group of like-minded women with whom they can fast, exercise, and provide mutual encouragement. Such a support network not only fosters strong relationships but also increases oxytocin levels in the brain, ultimately aiding in the balance of sex hormones.

Having discussed the four pillars of fasting considerations, the author acknowledges three essential lifestyle factors to consider when determining the fasting approach. One's relationship dynamics, schedule, and activity level should all influence the chosen fasting strategy.

Chapter four concludes with an uplifting reminder that women should avoid comparing their fasting schedules and outcomes to those of men.

Instead, fasting should be personalized to suit each woman's unique circumstances. Furthermore, the author encourages women to view setbacks as opportunities for learning, growth, and adaptation rather than becoming disheartened.

LESSONS AND KEY POINTS FROM THIS CHAPTER

1. Individualized healthcare emphasizes the importance of tailoring medical treatments and health approaches to each person's unique needs. This concept also applies to fasting.

2. Setting clear goals is crucial when engaging in fasting. Typical objectives include weight loss, hormone balance, or addressing specific health conditions.

3. Adapting the duration of fasting periods is advisable, taking into account hormonal fluctuations, social commitments, and personal health objectives.

4. Incorporating a diverse range of foods into your diet is essential to support a healthy gut and hormone balance.

5. Building a supportive community plays a significant role in fasting, as it provides a network of support and can enhance the release of oxytocin, a bonding hormone.

REFLECTION QUESTIONS

How can you tailor your fasts to your unique needs? What are some unique needs you may have that you want to consider?

What will you do if the unexpected occurs? Do you have a plan for what to do if you find yourself falling off the fasting wagon?

MILESTONE GOALS

1. What is your personal health goal for fasting?

2. Why is it important to vary the length of your fasts?

3. How many different foods do you think you eat in a month? How could you incorporate more healthy foods into your diet?

4. Do you know other women who fast? If not, how could you build a community with other women who fast?

ACTIONABLE MOVEMENTS

1. Determine your motivation for starting the fasting practice.

2. Initiate fasting by aiming for a sixteen-hour daily fasting window, while considering adjustments according to your hormonal cycle.

3. Incorporate a diverse range of foods into your daily diet to promote nutritional balance.

4. Establish a supportive network of like-minded women committed to fasting, allowing for mutual support and encouragement.

Record your reflections, insights, and observations on the concepts discussed earlier.

Use this space to brainstorm, sketch, or jot down any questions that arise in your mind. Make it a truly personal experience.

CH 6: FOODS THAT SUPPORT YOUR HORMONES

Summary

Chapter 6, titled "Foods that Support Your Hormones," introduces four key principles when it comes to food selection. These principles include:

1. **The Ingredients in your food**
2. **The glycemic load of your food**
3. **Eat a variety of foods**
4. **Vary your diet according to your menstrual cycle**

#1. The first principle, "Ingredients Matter," emphasizes the importance of reading ingredient labels. When examining labels, it is crucial to consider the number of ingredients (ideally fewer than five) and pay special attention to the first five listed. Additionally, scrutinize the presence of any toxins, types of oils, sugars, and flours. It is also essential to ensure the absence of artificial colors or flavors.

When it comes to supporting hormones, muscle building, and nurturing the gut biome, certain ingredients can play a significant role. Foods rich in good fats, seeds, nuts, legumes, fruits, and vegetables can support estrogen levels. Root and cruciferous vegetables, tropical and citrus fruits, as well as seeds and legumes, can promote progesterone production. For muscle building, prioritize proteins abundant in leucine, isoleucine, and valine amino acids. Options such as chicken, beef, fish, milk, cheese, eggs, tofu, and navy beans are favorable choices. To foster a healthy gut biome, consider incorporating probiotic, prebiotic, and polyphenol-rich foods. Fermented foods like sauerkraut, kimchi, pickles, yogurt, and kefir offer beneficial probiotics. Prebiotics can be found in onions, garlic, leeks, asparagus, hummus, chickpeas, and cashews. Lastly, polyphenol-rich foods, such as artichokes, Brussels sprouts, rosemary, thyme, basil, and dark chocolate, provide antioxidants.

By being mindful of ingredients and incorporating these supportive foods, you can contribute to hormone balance, muscle development, and gut health.

#2. The second principle of healthy eating addressed in the book is the glycemic load. The glycemic load is a numerical value ranging from 1 to 100, indicating the extent to which a food raises blood sugar levels. Foods with a glycemic load closer to 100 cause a more significant spike in blood sugar. To maintain stable blood sugar levels, the author recommends understanding macronutrients, which include carbohydrates, protein, and fats.

Carbohydrates: can be divided into two categories: simple and complex. Simple carbohydrates are typically found in processed foods and are considered man-made. On the other hand, complex carbohydrates are naturally occurring and can be found in fruits and vegetables. Complex carbohydrates are generally healthier and have a lower glycemic index compared to simple carbohydrates.

Protein: is another essential macronutrient that influences blood sugar levels in three ways. First, protein breaks down into glucose at a slower rate than carbohydrates. Secondly, protein is absorbed more slowly by the body than carbs. Lastly, protein provides a greater sense of satiety, helping you feel full for a longer duration.

Fat: is the third macronutrient. It can be classified into two types: good fats and bad fats. Good fats contain valuable nutrients for cellular health, while bad fats can cause inflammation in cells. Good fats have the additional benefit of stabilizing blood sugar levels and reducing hunger.
By understanding the glycemic load and the role of macronutrients, you can make informed choices to maintain balanced blood sugar levels and support overall health.

#3. The third principle of healthy eating emphasizes the significance of a diverse diet. The author suggests consuming a minimum of two hundred different types of foods within a month. These foods should fall under the categories of complex carbohydrates, proteins, or fats. It's worth noting that spices also contribute to dietary diversity and are an excellent way to enhance variety in your meals. The author recommends incorporating spices such as cardamom, cumin, star anise, turmeric, black pepper, cinnamon, and mustard seed into your diet to expand the range of flavors and nutrients you consume. By embracing a diverse selection of foods and spices, you can enhance the nutritional profile of your meals and enjoy a more varied and satisfying eating experience.

#4. The fourth and final principle of healthy eating emphasized in this book is the significance of cycling. Depending on the phase of your menstrual cycle, the author recommends specific dietary approaches. In the first part of your cycle, a ketobiotic diet is recommended. This term, coined by the author, refers to a diet with fewer than 50 grams of net carbs, primarily sourced from vegetables and greens. During this phase, it is advised to obtain 60% of your food from good fats and limit protein intake to no more than 75 grams.

As you approach the week before your period, the author suggests switching to a hormone-feasting diet. During this period, you should aim for around 150 net carbs, focusing on root vegetables and fruits. Protein consumption should be limited to no more than 50 grams, while healthy fats can be consumed liberally.

By aligning your diet with the different phases of your menstrual cycle, you can optimize your nutritional intake to support hormonal balance and overall well-being. It's important to note that these dietary recommendations are specific to the book's approach and may vary for individual needs and preferences. Consulting with a healthcare professional or nutritionist is always recommended for personalized dietary guidance.

At the conclusion of chapter six, a glimpse into chapter seven is provided. The author hints at the upcoming discussion on the fasting cycle, which will be further explored in the next chapter. This topic will serve as a continuation and expansion of the four food principles introduced in chapter six.

LESSONS AND KEY POINTS FROM THIS CHAPTER

1. The role of food in supporting your hormones cannot be overstated. When you go grocery shopping, it is crucial to carefully examine the ingredient labels on the food you purchase.

2. Understanding the glycemic index of a food provides valuable insight into how it affects your blood sugar levels and satiety.

3. To maintain a balanced diet, it is important to include a diverse range of complex carbohydrates, healthy fats, and nutritious proteins in your meals.

4. The ketobiotic diet and hormone-feasting diet are two distinct dietary approaches you should consider. The specific diet that suits you best will depend on your menstrual cycle and its unique demands.

REFLECTION QUESTIONS

During which fasts will you employ ketobiotic eating? Hormone feasting? Why?

Taking into account the four principles of eating, ask yourself how you plan to adjust your diet.

MILESTONE GOALS

1. What should you look for when reading the ingredients label on food?

2. Are foods with a lower or higher glycemic index better for you?

3. What are the three different macronutrients?

4. What are some spices you can add to your diet to increase the variety of foods you eat?

5. How many carbs should you eat on the ketobiotic diet? What about the hormone-feasting diet?

ACTIONABLE MOVEMENTS

Principle #1: Ingredients Matter
- Look at the ingredients list of the products you eat, not just the calories.
- Avoid foods with toxic ingredients that you don't recognize, such as sorbitol, sodium aluminum phosphate, and nitrates.
- Go for natural foods, such as potatoes instead of potato chips.
- Stick to the perimeter of the store for natural ingredients when shopping.

Principle #2: Glycemic Load Matters
- Measure your net carbohydrates, not the total.
- Swap out man-made carbohydrates for natural ones, which are complex and have more fiber.
- Combine carbohydrates with protein to prevent your blood sugar from spiking.
- Favor protein over carbohydrates, but don't eat too much protein.
- Choose good fats that nourish your cells, rather than bad fats that harm them.

Principle #3: Diversity Matters
- Aim to eat up to 200 different types of food in a month, falling into the categories of proteins, fats, and carbohydrates.
- Add spices to your diet, such as cardamom, cumin, turmeric, and rosemary.

Principle #4: Cycling Matters
- Know your hormonal patterns to cycle the types of foods you eat.
- During the first part of your cycle, eat ketobiotic foods that support low glucose and insulin, such as foods high in cholesterol and phytoestrogens.
- In the week before your period, switch to foods that support progesterone, such as root vegetables, cruciferous vegetables, tropical fruits, and legumes.
- Consume probiotic, prebiotic, and polyphenol-rich foods regularly to support your gut microbiome.

Record your reflections, insights, and observations on the concepts discussed earlier.

Use this space to brainstorm, sketch, or jot down any questions that arise in your mind. Make it a truly personal experience.

CH 7: THE FASTING CYCLE

Summary

Chapter seven, titled "The Fasting Cycle," emphasizes the importance of recognizing the unique fasting needs of women compared to men, considering their natural hormonal cycle. By aligning with this inherent cycle, the author introduces the concept of the Fasting Cycle as a way to optimize fasting benefits while honoring the natural hormonal rhythm.

The Fasting Cycle comprises three distinct phases: Power phase / Manifestation phase / Nurture phase

In the book, these phases are initially based on a thirty-day cycle. Nevertheless, the author emphasizes the importance of tailoring the fasting cycle to align with individual hormonal cycles. For cycles shorter than thirty days, it is recommended to continue following the last phase until the next menstrual period begins.

On the other hand, for cycles longer than thirty days, it is advised to start the fasting cycle from day one whenever the period commences. Women who do not experience a menstrual cycle or are postmenopausal can anticipate a dedicated reset plan outlined in the upcoming chapter.

#1. Power Phase. The initial phase of the fasting cycle is known as the power phase. In a thirty-day cycle, this phase occurs on days one through ten and repeats on days sixteen through nineteen. Within this phase, it is recommended to fast for a duration of thirteen to seventy-two hours. The longer fasts are particularly beneficial during days sixteen through nineteen when sex hormones are at their lowest point. These extended fasts facilitate autophagy, which aids in cellular healing. To optimize the benefits of autophagy and ketosis, it is advisable to follow a ketobiotic diet during this phase. This dietary approach helps maintain low levels of glucose and insulin, which in turn supports estrogen and helps regulate insulin levels.

#2. Manifestation phase. The next phase of the fasting cycle is known as the manifestation phase, which aligns with the ovulation period. In a thirty-day cycle, this phase occurs from days eleven through fifteen. During the manifestation phase, the book suggests fasting for thirteen to sixteen hours and following a hormone-feasting diet. This phase coincides with the peak levels of estrogen and testosterone, which contribute to feelings of strength and empowerment. Taking advantage of this hormonal surge, engaging in more challenging workouts, or initiating demanding work projects can enhance your potential for success during this phase.

#3. Nurture phase. The last phase of the fasting cycle is referred to as the nurture phase. It commences on day twenty of a thirty-day cycle and continues until the onset of a woman's menstrual period. During this phase, fasting is not advised. Instead, it is crucial to adhere to a hormone-feasting diet that prioritizes providing carbohydrates to support progesterone. However, the author emphasizes that opting for complex carbohydrates, rather than simple ones, is the preferred choice during this phase.

The author further advises minimizing stress during the nurture phase, as cortisol, the stress hormone, can have a negative impact on progesterone, the primary hormone during this phase. As chapter seven draws to a close, the author expresses hope that women feel motivated to embark on their fasting journey after understanding the fasting cycle.

The next chapter will delve into the comprehensive details of the thirty-day fasting reset, a specialized dietary approach for women engaging in fasting.

LESSONS AND KEY POINTS FROM THIS CHAPTER

1. The fasting cycle, designed by the author, is a fasting and eating schedule specifically tailored to women's natural cycle.

2. The power phase marks the first phase of the fasting cycle, spanning days 1-10 of a 30-day cycle. During this phase, fasting periods of 13-72 hours are recommended, accompanied by a ketobiotic diet.

3. Transitioning to the manifestation phase, which takes place on days 11-15, shorter

fasts of 13-16 hours are advised, while following a hormone-feasting diet.

4. Days 16-19 signal the return to the power phase. Similar to the initial power phase, fasting periods of 13-72 hours are encouraged, accompanied by the ketobiotic diet.

5. Finally, the nurture phase encompasses the period leading up to and including the first day of your menstrual cycle. During this phase, fasting is not recommended, and instead, focus on a hormone-feasting diet.

REFLECTION QUESTIONS

What are the stages of the fasting cycle? How can you fit this into your daily life? What routines will you have to adjust?

How do you time your fasts so that you can maximize their benefits? What does look like for your schedule? What challenges do you anticipate?

MILESTONE GOALS

1. What are the three phases of the fasting cycle?

2. What should you eat during the power phase?

3. Should you fast during the nurture phase?

4. How long should you fast during the manifestation phase?

ACTIONABLE MOVEMENTS

1. Familiarize yourself with the three phases of the fasting cycle: the power phase, the manifestation phase, and the nurture phase.

2. Determine where you are in your menstrual cycle and plan your fasting regimen accordingly. For example, during the power phase (days 1-10 and 16-19), consider longer fasts (13-72 hours) and follow a ketobiotic food style to focus on insulin and estrogen hormone levels and promote healing through autophagy and ketosis.

3. During the manifestation phase (days 11-15), focus on hormone feasting and supporting a healthy gut and liver. Try to fast for no longer than 15 hours and consume cruciferous vegetables, green leafy vegetables, sesame seeds, flaxseeds, fermented foods, salmon, apple varieties, berries, green teas, dandelion teas, and varied spices.

4. During the nurture phase (day 2 until the first day of your period), focus on reducing cortisol levels and caring for your progesterone levels to alleviate PMS symptoms. Avoid fasting during this phase and eat foods such as potatoes, sweet potatoes, yams, squashes, lentils and black beans, citrus fruits, tropical fruits, berries, pumpkin seeds, wild rice, brown rice, and quinoa.

5. Consider incorporating the fasting cycle as a lifestyle and using the 30-day reset plan outlined in the next chapter to maximize the benefits of fasting.

6. Stay aware of any changes in your body and adjust your fasting regimen accordingly. Consult with a healthcare professional if you have any concerns or medical conditions.

Record your reflections, insights, and observations on the concepts discussed earlier.

Use this space to brainstorm, sketch, or jot down any questions that arise in your mind. Make it a truly personal experience.

PART THREE: THE 30-DAY FASTING RESET

CH 8: 30-DAY FASTING RESET

Summary

Chapter eight, titled "30-Day Fasting Reset," presents a comprehensive plan for readers to embark on a thirty-day fasting journey. Before commencing the fasting reset, the author emphasizes the importance of tracking one's menstrual cycle, if applicable. Aligning the reset with the menstrual cycle is recommended, ensuring that if the cycle spans twenty-eight days, the reset duration matches accordingly. Acknowledging the potential challenges posed by fasting periods of thirteen to twenty hours, the author advises readers to prepare an action plan to overcome any difficulties that may arise.

In addition, the author encourages fasters to seek support by joining a community of like-minded individuals. A study conducted by Harvard over a span of eighty years, from 1938 to 2018, demonstrated a positive correlation between supportive relationships and overall well-being. For those who may not have access to a local fasting community, the author offers several free online communities that readers can join to find support and encouragement.

The book outlines that the thirty-day fasting reset is suitable for all women, regardless of their menstrual cycle. It highlights various health issues that this fast can potentially address, such as weight-loss resistance, insulin resistance, memory problems, menopause symptoms, low energy, hair loss, and digestive issues. Nevertheless, the author strongly advises consulting a healthcare professional before initiating any dietary or fasting modifications.

Prior to embarking on the thirty-day reset fast, the book provides a two-week pre-reset period for readers to follow. This preparatory phase incorporates three key criteria to be met:

1. **Foods to avoid**
2. **Foods to add**
3. **Compressing your eating window**

When planning meals during the two-week pre-reset period, it is important to avoid certain foods. These include bad oils, sugars, refined flour, and toxins. Bad oils encompass partially hydrogenated oils, cottonseed oil, corn oil, and vegetable oil. Sugars and flour should be avoided due to their negative impact on blood sugar levels and poor glycemic index, respectively. Additionally, it is crucial to be cautious of toxins such as artificial colors, artificial flavorings, dyes, Splenda, and NutraSweet.

Alongside the foods to avoid, there are several foods that should be incorporated into your diet during this pre-reset phase. These foods consist of good fats and healthy proteins. The book provides examples of good fats, including olive oil, avocado oil, MCT oils, grass-fed butter, and nut butter. These fats are encouraged as they can help reduce cravings. As for healthy proteins, the book suggests adding grass-fed beef, bison, turkey, chicken, and eggs to your diet.

The final requirement of the two-week pre-reset period is to start narrowing down your eating window. The eating window refers to the time span between your first and last meal of the day. The author suggests aiming for a thirteen-hour eating window as a target for readers. The book provides two strategies to achieve this goal.

The first strategy involves gradually delaying breakfast by one hour every two days until the desired eating window of thirteen hours is reached. The second strategy suggests advancing breakfast by one hour and pushing dinner back by one hour until the thirteen-hour eating window is achieved. To assist readers in reaching this goal, the author recommends consuming coffee or tea with MCT oil and cream in the morning to help reduce hunger.

Once the two-week pre-reset period is completed, it's time to embark on the thirty-day fasting reset. The fasting reset consists of four phases: Power Phase I, Manifestation Phase, Power Phase II, and Nurture Phase.

1. **Power Phase I** begins on day one and ends on day ten. During this time, you'll follow a ketobiotic diet. On the first four days, you should fast for thirteen hours. The fifth day includes a longer fast of fifteen hours, followed by seventeen-hour fasts on days six through ten.

2. The Manifestation Phase comes next on days eleven through fifteen. Diet in this phase should be hormone feasting, and fasts should last thirteen hours. After the Manifestation Phase is complete, a second power phase begins.

3. Power Phase II lasts from days sixteen through nineteen; the diet you should follow during this phase is ketobiotic. Fast lengths during this time are fifteen hours.

4. The Nurture Phase is the final phase of the thirty-day reset. This phase lasts from day twenty to day thirty and utilizes a hormone-feasting diet. During this time, you should not fast.

The author has developed the thirty-day reset to cater to individuals who are new to fasting. However, for experienced fasters, the book also offers a more advanced version of the thirty-day reset. This advanced reset follows the same four phases as the basic reset but with slightly longer fasting durations.

In the advanced reset, during Power Phase I, the recommended fast lengths are fifteen, twenty-four, and seventeen hours, respectively. The Manifestation phase entails fasts of fifteen hours. In Power Phase II, it is suggested to begin with a twenty-four-hour fast, followed by seventeen-hour fasts for the remaining duration of the phase. Lastly, during the Nurture Phase, the book advises fasting for thirteen hours.

Whether you opt for the basic or more advanced thirty-day fasting reset, the author suggests utilizing certain tools, known as biometrics, to assist you throughout the reset. These tools involve monitoring your blood sugar and ketone levels. However, it's important to note that using these tools during the thirty-day reset is not mandatory. If you choose to employ them, the author recommends taking your blood sugar three times a day and measuring your ketone levels twice a day.

The first measurement should be taken in the morning, immediately upon waking up. The second measurement should be conducted just before consuming your first meal of the day. According to the author, the second reading should ideally indicate lower blood sugar levels and higher ketone levels. This signifies that your body is effectively transitioning from burning ingested food to burning stored fats and sugars.

The third and final reading of the day should be taken two hours after eating, focusing solely on blood sugar levels. Ideally, the blood sugar levels between the second and third readings should remain relatively consistent, indicating good insulin sensitivity.

In conclusion, the author emphasizes the importance of finding enjoyment in the fasting process. While challenges may arise, having a supportive community to lean on is crucial for achieving success in fasting.

LESSONS AND KEY POINTS FROM THIS CHAPTER

1. Prior to embarking on your personal fasting journey, it is recommended to first undertake the author's two-week pre-fasting reset to facilitate the fasting process.

2. Throughout the fasting reset, endeavor to minimize the consumption of detrimental oils, sugars, flours, and toxins in your diet.

3. During the fasting reset, incorporate nourishing fats and wholesome proteins into your eating plan.

4. Condense your designated eating window to a span of thirteen hours.
5. Following the completion of the two-week fasting reset, you are now prepared to commence the fasting cycle.

REFLECTION QUESTIONS

What are some general rules for succeeding at your fasts? What challenges do you anticipate?

Why do you need to use intermittent fasts during the 30-day reset?

What ways do you think fasting will need to accommodate your schedule? How do you plan to be flexible?

MILESTONE GOALS

1. Based on your social life and calendar, when would be a good time for you to start the two-week pre-reset?

2. What are some toxins you should remove from your diet?

3. What good fats and healthy proteins should you add to your diet?

4. What is your current eating window (time between your first and last meal)? How long should this eating window be?

5. Do you have a blood sugar monitor and ketone monitor to help your fasts? If not, do you plan on getting one?

ACTIONABLE MOVEMENTS

1. Begin tracking your menstrual cycle if you have one.

2. Remove the foods to avoid from your diet and begin incorporating healthy proteins and good fats.

3. Move our breakfast back by an hour until you've reached a thirteen-hour fasting window.

4. Look at your calendar and pick a time to start the thirty-day fasting reset.

5. Decide if you want to follow the basic or advanced fasting reset.

Remember to have compassion towards yourself and understand that fasting can be challenging. With proper preparation and support, you can successfully complete the 30-Day Fasting Reset plan and improve your health.

Record your reflections, insights, and observations on the concepts discussed earlier.

Use this space to brainstorm, sketch, or jot down any questions that arise in your mind. Make it a truly personal experience.

CH 9: HOW TO BREAK A FAST

Summary

In the ninth chapter titled "how to break a fast", the author delves into the process of concluding a fast. While acknowledging the scarcity of research on optimal post-fast eating, the author shares her personal experimentation and highlights four prevalent strategies for breaking a fast. These strategies are as follows:

1. Incorporating fast-breaking foods to restore and rebalance the gut's microbiome.
2. Consuming fast-breaking foods that aid in muscle building and recovery.
3. Opting for fast-breaking foods that promote fat-burning and metabolic activation.
4. Choosing to eat whatever appeals to you in the moment.

By exploring these various approaches, the author aims to provide readers with insights and options for effectively concluding their fasting periods.

The initial strategy for breaking a fast focuses on resetting the microbiome, and it is particularly suitable for individuals seeking to achieve this goal. The author suggests consuming foods rich in probiotics, prebiotics, and polyphenols. Within this section, the author shares her preferred fast-breaking meal for promoting gut health, which consists of half an avocado paired with one cup of sauerkraut, complemented by a sprinkle of pumpkin seeds and flaxseed oil. Additionally, the author recommends incorporating other beneficial foods into the post-fast routine, such as fermented yogurts, bone broth, kombucha, seeds, and seed oils. These choices can contribute to the desired microbiome reset and enhance overall gut well-being.

The next fast-breaking method is designed for people who are trying to build muscle. The author addresses a prevalent misconception that fasting leads to muscle loss. However, the author assures readers that this is not the case, as muscles may temporarily appear smaller due to the release of stored sugars during fasting. To maintain and promote muscle growth after a fast, it is crucial to consume a protein-rich meal. The book suggests various protein options, such as eggs, beef sticks/jerky, chicken breast, and protein shakes derived from peas, hemp, or whey.

The third method of breaking a fast is particularly beneficial for those seeking to burn fat. The author emphasizes that fats help stabilize blood sugar levels, making them an advantageous choice to conclude a fast. However, the book highlights that not all fats will break a fast for everyone. Factors such as microbiome diversity and insulin resistance can influence the impact of fats on fasting. To determine whether a particular fat breaks your fast, the author recommends measuring your blood pressure before consuming the food or beverage in question and then measuring it again thirty minutes later. If your blood sugar remains consistent between these measurements, it indicates that the fat consumed did not break your fast.

There are several fats commonly known not to break a fast, including supplements and medication, black coffee and coffee with full-fat cream, teas, flaxseed oil, MCT oil, mineral water, and small portions of nut butter. However, the author advises readers to personally test these fats before incorporating them into their fasting routine.

The last approach to breaking a fast involves consuming whatever tastes best to you. However, the author cautions against relying solely on this strategy. While it may provide immediate satisfaction, it can limit the healing effects of the fast. To fully maximize the benefits of fasting, the author recommends following another fast-breaking strategy.

For fasts lasting longer than forty-eight hours, the author provides a four-step eating plan to gradually reintroduce food and end the fast.

1. Sip a cup of bone broth.
2. Wait an hour, then eat a meal full of probiotics and good fat.
3. After waiting another hour, eat some steamed vegetables. If you feel bloated after this meal, it is likely due to gut issues. If this is the case for you, the author recommends following the advice in the book to improve your gut microbiome.
4. Eat a meal with plenty of animal protein, at least thirty grams.

No matter how you choose to end a fast, the author closes this chapter with the reminder that better food choices after a fast will equate to more health benefits and faster progress toward your health goals.

LESSONS AND KEY POINTS FROM THIS CHAPTER

1. When breaking a fast, prioritize foods that align with your health goals.

2. For enhancing gut health, opt for foods abundant in polyphenols, probiotics, and prebiotics to break your fast.

3. If your goal is to build muscle, break your fast with a protein-rich meal.

4. Keep in mind that not all fats will break your fast, especially when aiming to burn fat. Utilize a blood sugar monitor to identify which fats have an impact on your fasting state.

5. Avoid breaking your fast with whatever appeals to your taste buds as it may diminish the health advantages of fasting.

REFLECTION QUESTIONS

What foods do you plan to eat at the end of a fast? Why?

Consider foods that may pull you out of a fasted state to make sure you are reaping the benefits of longer fasts.

MILESTONE GOALS

1. What goals do you have for fasting?

_____

_____

_____

2. Based on your health goals, what should you eat to break a fast?

_____

_____

3. Does eating full-fat cream, nut butter, and other fats always break a fast?

4. How should you break a 48-hour fast?

ACTIONABLE MOVEMENTS

1. Test your blood sugar before and after eating some of the good fats listed in this chapter to see if it impacts your blood sugar.

2. Create a plan to break your fast, tailoring it to your health goals.

3. If you want to build muscle, plan a meal full of protein to break your fast.

4. If you want to improve your gut health, plan a meal full of probiotics, prebiotics, and polyphenols to break your fast.

Record your reflections, insights, and observations on the concepts discussed earlier.

Use this space to brainstorm, sketch, or jot down any questions that arise in your mind. Make it a truly personal experience.

CH 10: HACKS THAT MADE FASTING EFFORTLESS

Summary

In the tenth chapter of this book, titled "Hacks that Make Fasting Effortless," the author shares a range of strategies to make fasting more manageable for readers. The chapter starts with an important reminder that prioritizing health can take time. The author encourages readers to embrace fasting as a practice, celebrating their progress and acknowledging that any fasting duration is better than none at all. It's emphasized to approach fasting with curiosity and view setbacks as opportunities for growth and learning. The chapter presents the following hacks to facilitate the fasting experience:

1. Differentiate between hunger and boredom: It's essential to recognize whether you're truly hungry or simply seeking distraction from boredom. If it's boredom, the author suggests engaging in activities that boost dopamine, such as playing sports or connecting with a friend. However, if genuine hunger arises and you wish to continue fasting, the author recommends using a mineral pack. LMNT and Redmond are mentioned as the author's preferred brands. Alternatively, incorporating fasting snacks like MCT oil or cream in coffee or tea can help satiate hunger. Adding a drink with prebiotic powder can also support your gut microbiome and help minimize cravings.

2. Minimize the effects of toxin removal: During fasting, your body eliminates toxins, which can sometimes lead to flu-like symptoms. To mitigate these feelings, the book suggests various practices. Dry brushing, sweating through physical activity or saunas, lymph massages, and Epsom salt baths are mentioned as effective ways to support the detoxification process. Additionally, jumping on a trampoline is highlighted as a beneficial activity that aids the lymphatic system. Lastly, consuming binders like zeolite or activated charcoal can assist your body in removing toxins, reducing the likelihood of experiencing flu-like symptoms.

3. Utilize biometrics: Measuring blood sugar and ketones can provide valuable insights during fasting. The author suggests following the protocol outlined in the previous chapter for taking these measurements. To lower blood sugar levels and promote ketosis, the author recommends incorporating longer fasts, varying fast lengths, and avoiding processed foods. Supporting liver function through methods such as castor oil packs, coffee enemas, infrared saunas, essential oils, bitter lettuce, and dandelion teas can further aid in reducing blood sugar and facilitating ketone burning. Additionally, utilizing a DUTCH hormone test or taking supplements to support adrenal health and eliminate toxins from your lifestyle can contribute to lowering blood sugar and promoting ketosis.

4. Enhance detoxification: To optimize the body's detoxification process, the author suggests engaging in activities that promote sweating, staying well-hydrated, practicing dry brushing, and performing lymphatic massages. It's worth noting that some women may experience irregularities in their menstrual cycles during the detoxification phase. If this occurs, the author recommends continuing with the thirty-day reset fast, as each person's detoxification journey is unique.

The remaining hacks in this chapter are tailored to specific health concerns. The book recommends varying your fasting lengths and adding supplements if you lose hair during a fast. Suppose you experience fatigue while fasting. Red light therapy and hyperbaric chambers can reduce fatigue by supporting your mitochondria.

If you are taking medication, it is generally recommended to take it during your designated eating window. However, it is important to consult with your doctor before making any changes to your medication or discussing how fasting may affect your treatment plan. On the other hand, supplements can be taken at any time, but it is advisable to pause their intake during a three-day water fast or as guided by healthcare professionals.

For individuals who experience cravings, the book suggests that these cravings may be attributed to "bad" bacteria in the gut. Continuing with fasting and extending the fasting period can aid in reducing these harmful bacteria and promoting the growth of beneficial bacteria, thus helping to alleviate cravings.

Some individuals may notice changes in their sleep patterns during fasting. It is common to require less sleep while fasting. However, if you experience discomfort while sleeping, the author recommends considering the use of a magnesium supplement or using CBD lotions and tinctures to help alleviate any discomfort.

Remember to consult with a healthcare professional for personalized advice regarding medication, supplements, and any changes to your fasting routine or sleep patterns.

If you are a woman recovering from a hysterectomy, the book recommends implementing the thirty-day fasting reset as a means to promote hormone balance. In the case of individuals with a thyroid condition, the author dispels the notion that fasting leads to a decrease in thyroid hormones. Instead, the author explains that the T3 hormone may temporarily decrease during fasting but returns to normal levels after eating. Regarding individuals with adrenal fatigue, fasting can potentially offer relief by helping to stabilize blood sugar levels.

The book advises against fasting for pregnant women due to the release of toxins, which should be avoided for the well-being of the baby. For breastfeeding mothers, fasts should be limited to thirteen hours in order to minimize toxin exposure. However, it is important for readers in these situations to consult with their healthcare provider. Similarly, for individuals with diabetes or a history of eating disorders, it is recommended to have a conversation with their doctor. While fasting can have benefits for individuals with diabetes or those in recovery from an eating disorder, consulting with a healthcare professional ensures a safe fasting experience.

After discussing the hacks in this chapter, the author encourages readers to seek out her communities. These include free Facebook groups, online communities, and a YouTube channel, where readers can connect with other fasting enthusiasts, expand their knowledge about fasting, and seek answers to any additional questions they may have.

LESSONS AND KEY POINTS FROM THIS CHAPTER

1. Develop the ability to distinguish between boredom and hunger while fasting.

2. Incorporate practices like dry brushing, Epsom salt baths, lymph massages, and trampoline exercises to alleviate detoxification symptoms.

3. Utilize blood sugar and ketone monitors to personalize your fasting approach according to your body's needs.

4. If you experience a missed period during fasting, it may be attributed to detoxification processes in your body. In such cases, continue with the fasting regimen and employ additional hacks to mitigate detox symptoms.

MILESTONE GOALS

1. While fasting, have you experienced any negative symptoms?

2. Do you have any specific conditions that fasting could address? If so, what examples does the author provide on how fasting helps your condition?

3. How can you improve your liver function and help your body detox?

4. What are some ways to minimize hunger while fasting?

ACTIONABLE MOVEMENTS

1. When hunger arises during a fast, pause and inquire whether it stems from genuine hunger or a mere sense of boredom.

2. Select one or more detoxification hacks from the book and incorporate them into your daily or weekly routine to enhance your body's detox processes.

3. Pay attention to any health issues that may arise during fasting and utilize the relevant hacks recommended in the book to address these concerns effectively.

4. If you are pregnant, breastfeeding, have diabetes, have a history of an eating disorder, or harbor any uncertainties about fasting, it is crucial to consult with your doctor for guidance and advice.

Record your reflections, insights, and observations on the concepts discussed earlier.

Use this space to brainstorm, sketch, or jot down any questions that arise in your mind. Make it a truly personal experience.

RECIPES

The book concludes with its eleventh chapter, entirely devoted to a delightful collection of recipes. The author commences the chapter by reminding readers of the importance of embracing food variety and exploring new culinary adventures. The recipes in this chapter are thoughtfully organized into three sections: ketobiotic, hormone feasting, and breaking your fast.

Within the ketobiotic section, you'll discover an array of enticing recipes, including loaded hummus bowls, shakshuka adorned with pickled onions and avocado, kimchi salad crowned with crisped chickpeas, and a delectable frittata featuring prosciutto, spinach, and asparagus.

Moving on to the hormone feasting section, you'll find a tantalizing selection of recipes, such as white bean and kale soups, herb-infused steaks accompanied by a side of mashed potatoes and vegetables, sweet potatoes stuffed with chipotle black beans, hash browns crafted from sweet potatoes, and quinoa tabouli, among other tempting creations.

Finally, the last section presents recipes specifically designed to break your fast, offering an array of delightful meals. Indulge in a luscious smoothie crafted with avocado and berries, savor burger patties topped with creamy guacamole, relish the combination of avocado and tuna salad, treat yourself to a refreshing strawberry and mint flavored kefir smoothie, or indulge in a heavenly vanilla chia pudding adorned with chocolate and berries. These recipes are tailored to provide you with a satisfying experience as you conclude your fasting journey.

AFTERWARD & APPENDICES

The book concludes with a heartfelt afterword from the author, where she shares an inspiring story about Lana, a woman who defied the odds by successfully battling metastatic breast cancer and living for another eleven years through significant lifestyle changes. The author then expresses her own passion for fasting and her excitement about witnessing women embrace healthy transformations, particularly during the challenging times of the COVID-19 pandemic. She concludes the book with a heartfelt desire to see more women empowered to take control of their health and wholeheartedly embrace the fasting lifestyle.

In the final pages, you will find three informative appendices. Appendix A serves as a comprehensive glossary, providing definitions of frequently used fasting terms to enhance your understanding. Appendix B offers a valuable compilation of foods that are beneficial for your health, including probiotic-rich foods, nourishing fats, and wholesome sources of protein.

Lastly, Appendix C delves into specific fasting protocols tailored to address various health concerns, such as infertility, chronic fatigue, depression, and type II diabetes. This appendix serves as a valuable resource, providing targeted guidance for individuals seeking to address specific health conditions through fasting.

With these appendices, the author provides additional knowledge and practical tools to support your fasting journey and overall well-being.

THOUGHT PROVOKING DISCUSSION QUESTIONS

Has the author successfully persuaded you to explore fasting?

_____

_____

_____

_____

Have you previously engaged in fasting? If so, what was the duration and schedule of your fasting experience? Did you adhere to a consistent daily fasting routine?

_____

_____

_____

What specific health improvements do you aspire to achieve through fasting?

Now that you possess knowledge about the hormonal fluctuations during your menstrual cycle, do you plan to adjust your work and lifestyle accordingly to align with these changes?

What was the most surprising thing you learned from this book?

Do you hold any disagreements with the author's viewpoints? If so, which aspects and what are your reasons?

How do you plan to tackle challenges that may arise while fasting?

How will you go about establishing a community of women with whom you can engage in fasting together?

Which lifestyle changes mentioned in the book excite you the most?

Are you more eager about indulging in metabiotic or hormone-feasting meals?

Can you explain the concept of hormonal hierarchy? Which hormone is considered the key hormone in this hierarchy?

What are the four distinct phases of the thirty-day fasting reset?

What food choices do you intend to make when breaking a fast?

Did the book persuade you to eliminate certain toxins from your life? If so, what strategies do you plan to employ for toxin removal?

Do you believe it is feasible for you to consume two hundred unique foods within a month? If yes, please explain why, and if not, please elaborate on your reasoning.

ACTIONABLE STEPS TO INTEGRATE FASTING INTO YOUR DAILY LIFE

A Step-by-step Plan for Implementing the Insights Presented in this Book

1. Eliminate the five diet mistakes outlined in Chapter X from your eating habits.

2. Deepen your understanding of hormonal fluctuations throughout your menstrual cycle and their effects on your body. Chapters 2 and 4 can serve as a helpful review if needed.

3. Gain a comprehensive understanding of metabolic switching and its significance for women. If you need a refresher, consult Chapter 3.

4. Prior to making any dietary or lifestyle changes, it is advisable to consult with your healthcare provider.

5. Whenever feasible, eliminate toxins, unhealthy oils, sugars, flour, and simple carbohydrates from your diet. Refer to Chapter 6 for detailed information on these food items.

6. Embrace a diverse range of foods in your diet, with a particular focus on fruits, vegetables, complex carbohydrates, beneficial fats, and nutritious

proteins. Chapter 6 provides examples of such nourishing foods.

7. If you experience menstrual cycles, start tracking your cycle regularly.

8. Begin the two-week pre-fasting reset as outlined in Chapter 7.

9. Commence the thirty-day fasting reset, scheduling it in accordance with your menstrual cycle if applicable. For a quick recap, refer to Chapter 8.

10. Choose the most suitable foods to break your fast, taking into account your specific health goals. Chapter 9 offers a comprehensive list of such foods.

11. If you encounter challenges or have specific health conditions, incorporate the fasting hacks detailed in Chapter 10.

ABOUT US.

Peakread Publishing emerged from a collective of passionate readers who shared a common desire for personal growth and continuous learning. These individuals were avid readers, attending seminars and devouring books, but they soon encountered a common challenge: the overwhelming abundance of information available and the difficulty of retaining and applying it all.

Driven by their shared pursuit of knowledge, they decided to tackle this problem head-on. Thus, Peakread Publishing was born—a brand dedicated to providing the finest summary books and workbooks available on the market. Their ultimate vision was to distill the core concepts and takeaways from the most impactful books and seminars, enabling others to learn and develop more efficiently and effectively.

The team behind Peakread Publishing poured their hearts and souls into meticulously curating the most valuable content, transforming it into easily digestible summaries and workbooks. Their commitment to excellence led them to continuously test and refine their methods until they perfected their approach, establishing an association renowned for its unmatched quality and unwavering reliability.

The driving force behind Peakread Publishing was the firm belief that learning and personal development should be accessible to everyone, regardless of how busy their lives may be. Their aim was to empower individuals with the insights and knowledge capable of transforming their lives, delivering easy-to-access resources that could be integrated seamlessly into any lifestyle.

As the association flourished, it garnered a global reputation as the foremost provider of summary books and workbooks. It became the trusted resource that readers and learners worldwide turned to for discovering fresh ideas, gaining new perspectives, and acquiring vital skills. However, the true measure of success for Peakread Publishing was in the positive changes and actions that individuals took as a result of their publications.

Today, Peakread Publishing stands tall as the unrivaled leader in the market of summary books and workbooks. Its products have played an instrumental role in enabling countless individuals to learn, grow, and achieve their goals. The brand's story serves as a testament to the boundless power of learning and the incredible potential that resides within each and every individual, waiting to be harnessed and transformed.

At Peakread Publishing, we are always eager to improve and refine our offerings. Your suggestions and feedback are invaluable to us. We welcome any advice or recommendations you may have and invite you to reach out to us via email. Your input is highly valued, and we look forward to hearing from you as we continue on our mission to empower individuals through the gift of knowledge and learning.

peakreadpublishing@gmail.com

Thank you!

We are constantly striving to provide the ideal experience for the community, and your input helps us to define that experience. So we kindly ask you when you have free time take a minute to post a review on Amazon.

Thank you for helping us support our passions.

TO LEAVE A REVIEW, JUST SCAN THE QR CODE BELOW:

OR YOU CAN GO TO:

amazon.com/review/create-review/

Made in the USA
Las Vegas, NV
13 July 2023

74711491R00057